DAVID A. ADLER

Kindergarten MA+H

WORKBOOK

Illustrated by Edward Miller

HOLIDAY HOUSE · NEW YORK

Dear Parents and Teachers,

I'm a former math teacher and have been a published author for many years. I have happily combined my two careers in writing many introductory math books for young children. As a teacher, I knew that children need to not just learn basic math skills and concepts, but to practice them, and practice them again.

In this *Kindergarten Math Workbook*, artist Edward Miller and I used the common core curriculum and math standards for kindergartners to produce a workbook that makes learning and practicing simple math concepts clear and entertaining. This book gives young students a chance to practice writing numbers up to 20, do basic addition and subtraction, learn about place value, make comparisons, and learn simple positioning words.

Edward and I hope this book will provide enjoyment for young learners while they practice and learn, just as we have enjoyed bringing it to you.

Thank you,

David A. Adler

To My Grandson Ari —DAA

David A. Adler's First Grade Math Workbook copyright © 2022 by Holiday House Publishing, Inc.
Illustrations copyright © 2022 by Edward Miller III

HOLIDAY HOUSE is registered in the U.S. Patent and Trademark Office.
Printed and bound in May 2022 at Toppan Leefung, DongGuan, China.
The artwork was created digitally.
www.holidayhouse.com
First Edition
1 3 5 7 9 10 8 6 4 2

ISBN: 978-0-8234-5313-9 (workbook)

Contents

Counting and Numbers

Trace the numbers.

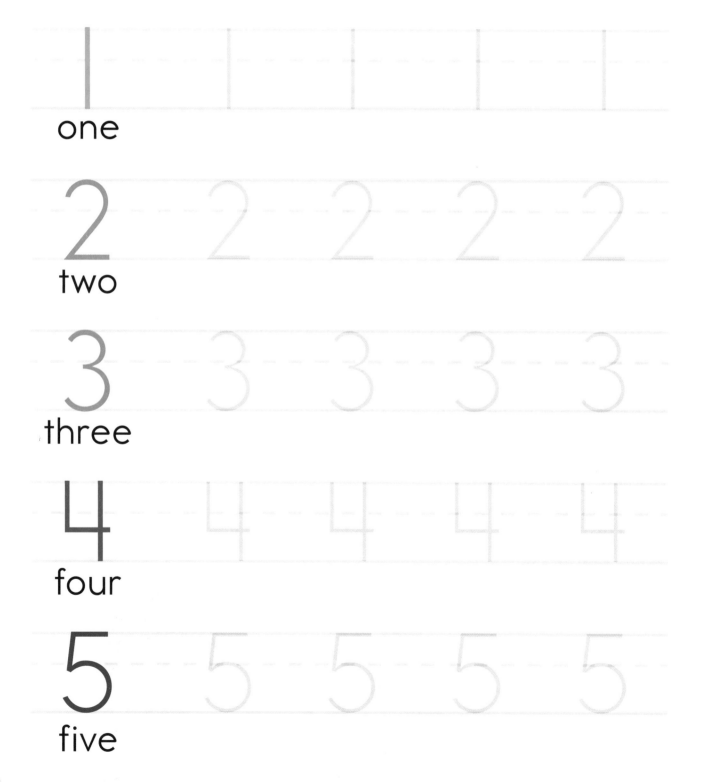

1 one

2 two

3 three

4 four

5 five

1 2 3 4 5

Count the number of items in
each row and write the number.

Trace the numbers.

6 six

7 seven

8 eight

9 nine

10 ten

1 2 3 4 5 6 7 8 9 10

Count the number of items in
each row and write the number.

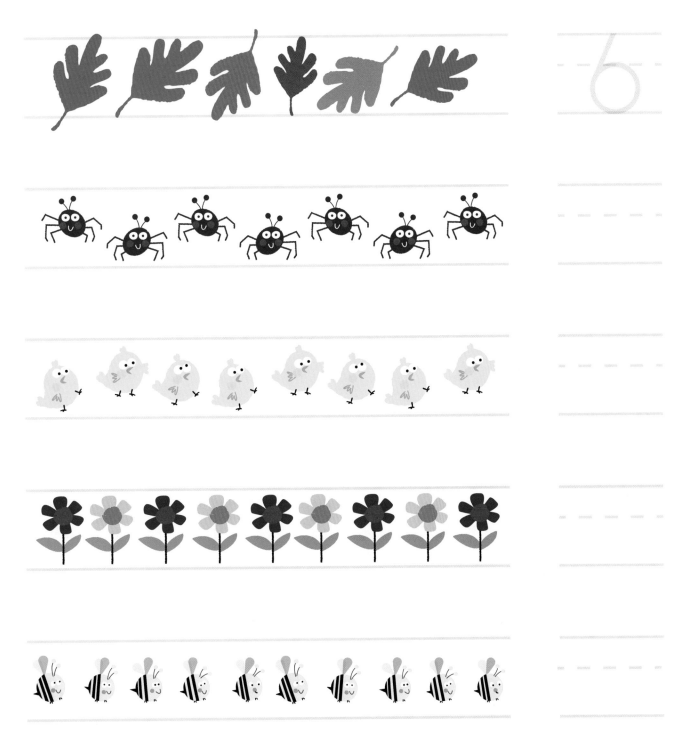

6

4

Trace the numbers.

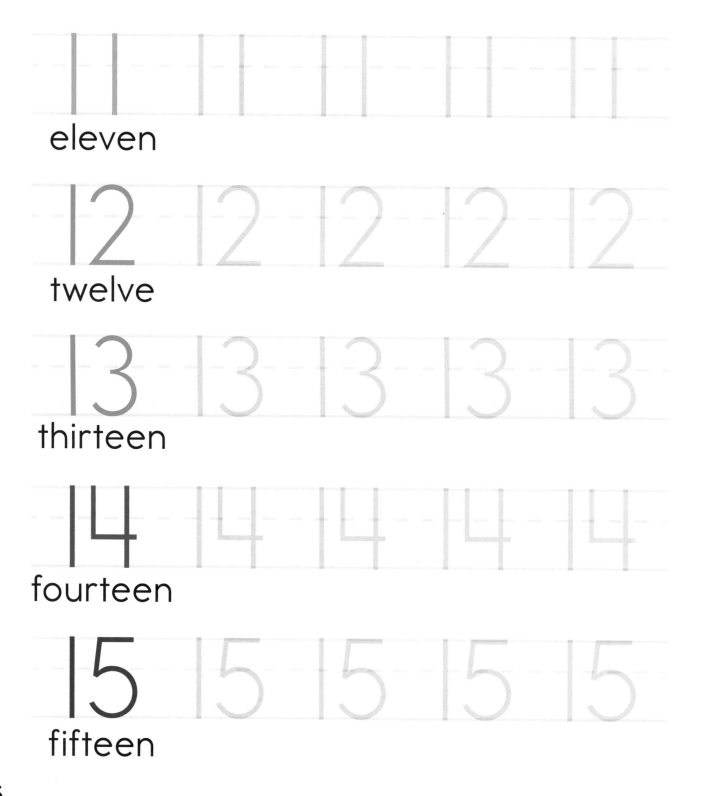

eleven

twelve

thirteen

fourteen

fifteen

1 2 3 4 5 6 7 8 9 10 11 12 13 14 15

Count the number of items in
each row and write the number.

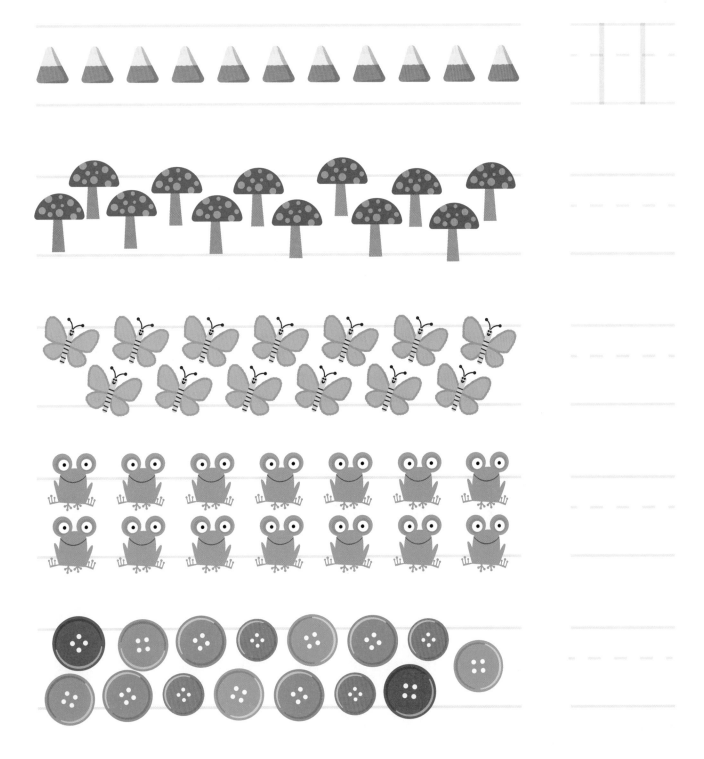

Trace the numbers.

16
sixteen

17
seventeen

18
eighteen

19
nineteen

20
twenty

10 11 12 13 14 15 16 17 18 19 20

Count the number of items in
each row and write the number.

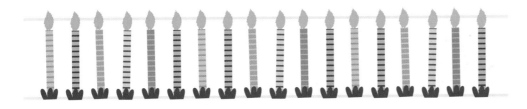

How many?

Count the objects and tell us how many there are. Write your answers in the boxes.

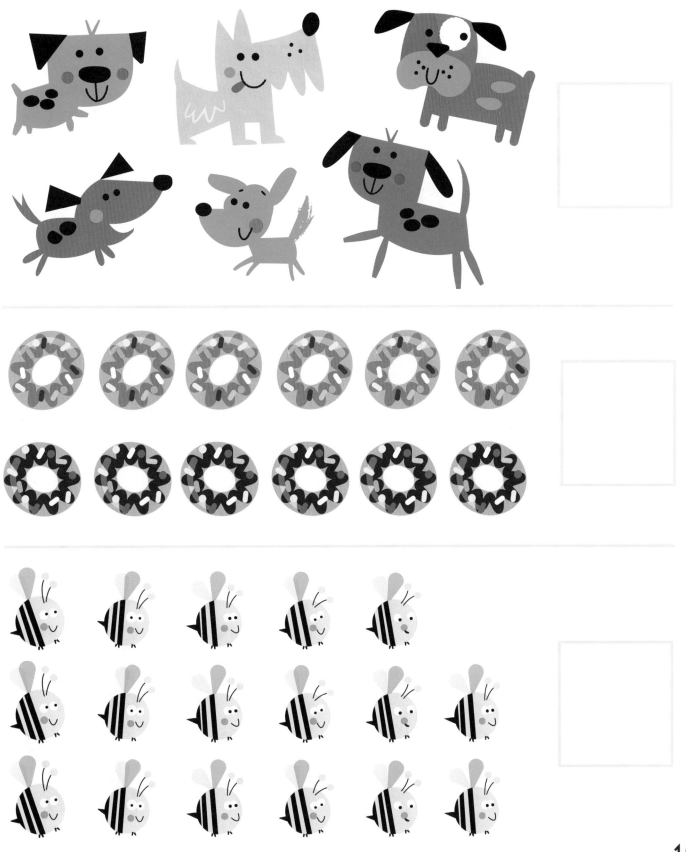

Which has more?

Circle the group that has **more**.

Circle the group that has **more**.

Circle the group that has **more**.

Circle the group that has **more**.

Which has less?

Circle the group that has **less**.

Circle the group that has **less**.

Circle the group that has **less**.

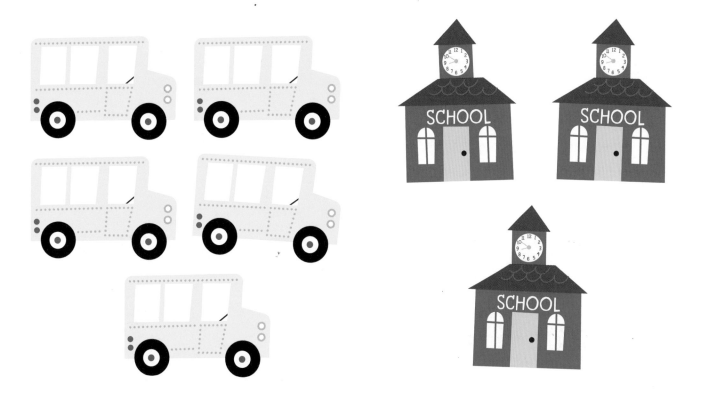

Circle the group that has **less**.

Which number is bigger?
Circle the bigger number in each box.

5
five

7
seven

13
thirteen

15
fifteen

Which number is smaller?

Circle the smaller number in each box.

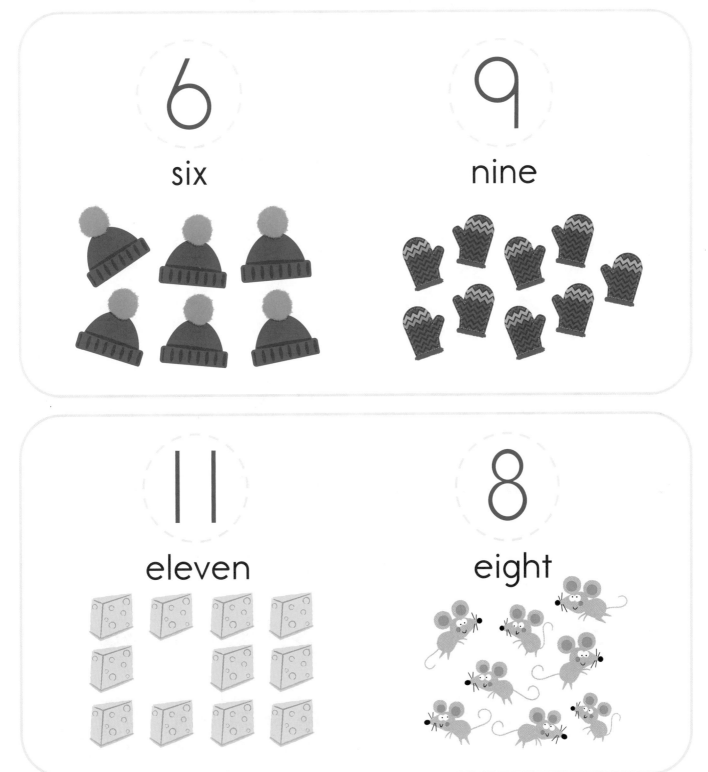

6
six

9
nine

11
eleven

8
eight

How many is 100?

1	2	3	4	5	6	7	8	9	10
11	12	13	14	15	16	17	18	19	20
21	22	23	24	25	26	27	28	29	30
31	32	33	34	35	36	37	38	39	40
41	42	43	44	45	46	47	48	49	50
51	52	53	54	55	56	57	58	59	60
61	62	63	64	65	66	67	68	69	70
71	72	73	74	75	76	77	78	79	80
81	82	83	84	85	86	87	88	89	90
91	92	93	94	95	96	97	98	99	100

Fill in the missing numbers.

1   2   3   4   5   6   7   ☐   9   10

11   12   13   14   ☐   16   17   18   ☐   20

21   22   23   ☐   25   26   27   28   29   30

31   ☐   33   34   35   36   ☐   38   39   40

☐   42   43   44   45   46   47   48   49   50

51   52   53   54   ☐   56   57   58   59   ☐

61   62   63   ☐   65   66   67   ☐   69   70

☐   72   73   74   75   76   77   78   79   80

81   82   83   84   ☐   86   ☐   88   89   90

91   92   ☐   94   95   96   97   98   99   100

Count to 100 by 10s.

1	2	3	4	5	6	7	8	9	**10**
11	12	13	14	15	16	17	18	19	**20**
21	22	23	24	25	26	27	28	29	**30**
31	32	33	34	35	36	37	38	39	**40**
41	42	43	44	45	46	47	48	49	**50**
51	52	53	54	55	56	57	58	59	**60**
61	62	63	64	65	66	67	68	69	**70**
71	72	73	74	75	76	77	78	79	**80**
81	82	83	84	85	86	87	88	89	**90**
91	92	93	94	95	96	97	98	99	**100**

Write the tens in the box at the end of each row.

★	★	★	★	★	★	★	★	★	
1	2	3	4	5	6	7	8	9	10

●	●	●	●	●	●	●	●	●	
11	12	13	14	15	16	17	18	19	

■	■	■	■	■	■	■	■	■	
21	22	23	24	25	26	27	28	29	

▲	▲	▲	▲	▲	▲	▲	▲	▲	
31	32	33	34	35	36	37	38	39	

●	●	●	●	●	●	●	●	●	
41	42	43	44	45	46	47	48	49	

✖	✖	✖	✖	✖	✖	✖	✖	✖	
51	52	53	54	55	56	57	58	59	

◆	◆	◆	◆	◆	◆	◆	◆	◆	
61	62	63	64	65	66	67	68	69	

◉	◉	◉	◉	◉	◉	◉	◉	◉	
71	72	73	74	75	76	77	78	79	

◗	◗	◗	◗	◗	◗	◗	◗	◗	
81	82	83	84	85	86	87	88	89	

▬	▬	▬	▬	▬	▬	▬	▬	▬	
91	92	93	94	95	96	97	98	99	

20

How many is 100?

10	20	30	40	50
ten	twenty	thirty	forty	fifty
60	70	80	90	100
sixty	seventy	eighty	ninety	one hundred

Trace the numbers.

10   20   30   40   50

60   70   80   90   100

10   20   30   40   50

60   70   80   90   100

tens

1	2	3	4	5	6	7	8	9	**10**
11	12	13	14	15	16	17	18	19	**20**
21	22	23	24	25	26	27	28	29	**30**
31	32	33	34	35	36	37	38	39	**40**
41	42	43	44	45	46	47	48	49	**50**
51	52	53	54	55	56	57	58	59	**60**
61	62	63	64	65	66	67	68	69	**70**
71	72	73	74	75	76	77	78	79	**80**
81	82	83	84	85	86	87	88	89	**90**
91	92	93	94	95	96	97	98	99	**100**

Learn to add!

Count the stars. Write the number in the first empty box. Draw one more star. Count the stars again. Now write the total number in the second box. You have just added by one.

Do the same with the circles, triangles, diamonds, and hearts that follow.

$$3 + 1 = 4$$

$$\boxed{} + 1 = \boxed{}$$

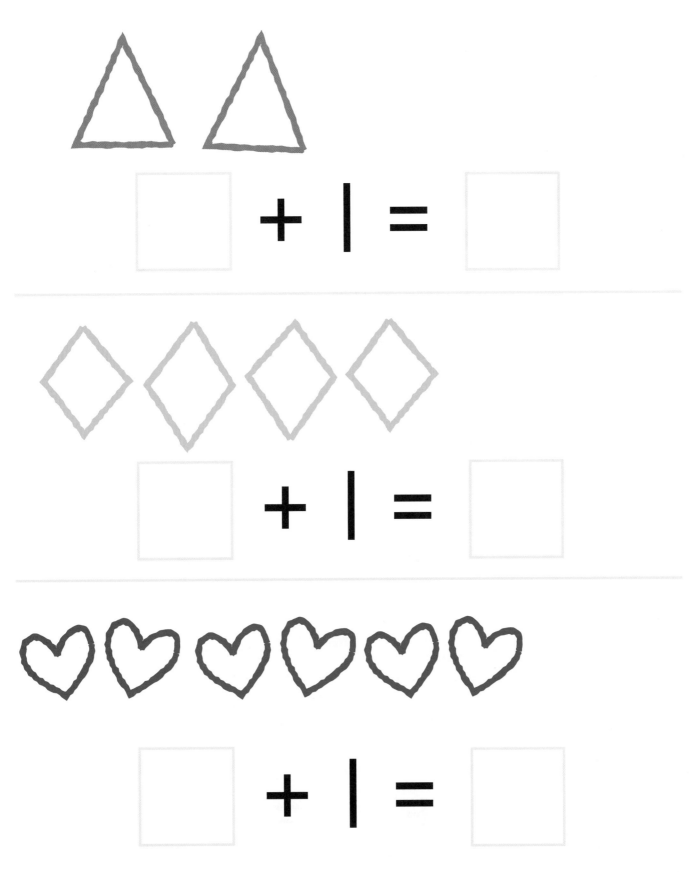

When we add numbers together, we put a **+** between them. We put a **=** before the total number.

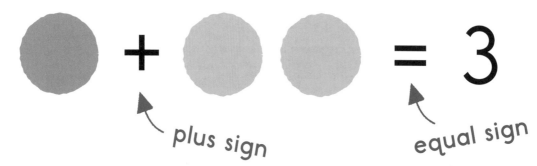

plus sign

equal sign

Count each of the different shapes then add them together.

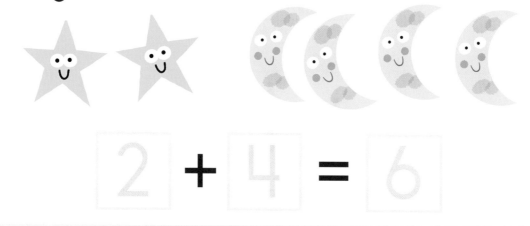

$2 + 4 = 6$

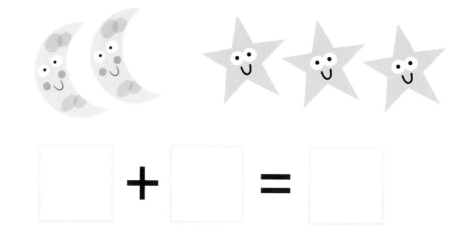

$\square + \square = \square$

Learn to subtract!

When we subtract, we put a **−** between the numbers.

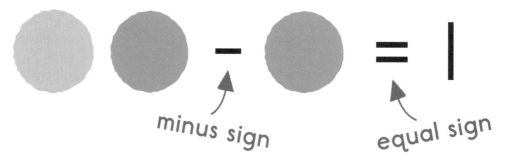

minus sign

equal sign

Count the pictures in each row. Put the number in the first box. Cross one picture out and count the remaining pictures. Don't count the one you crossed out. You have just subtracted by one.

3 − 1 = 2

− =

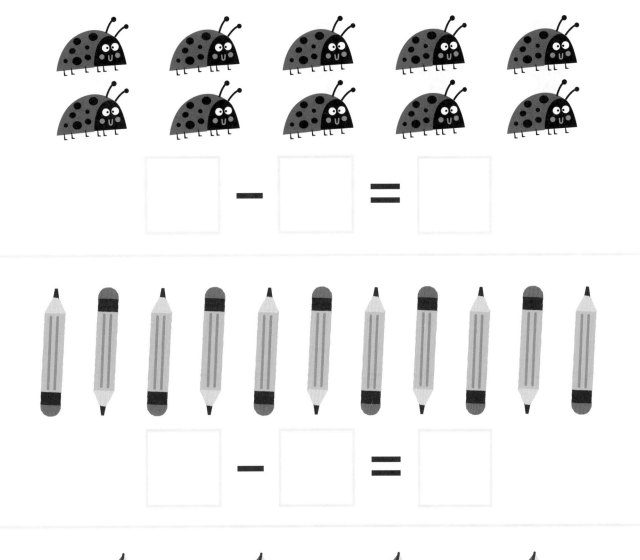

☐ − ☐ = ☐

☐ − ☐ = ☐

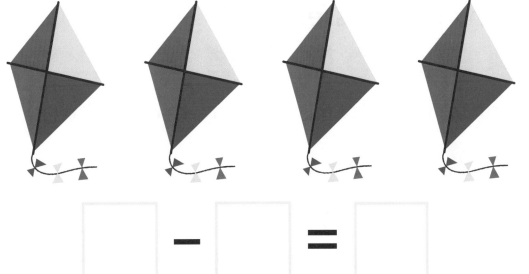

☐ − ☐ = ☐

28

How many stars are there?

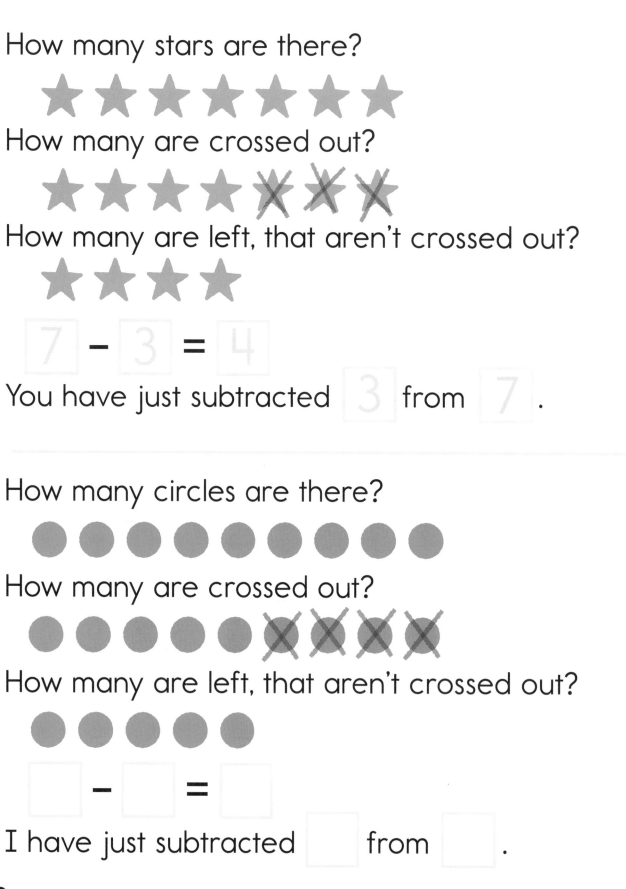

How many are crossed out?

How many are left, that aren't crossed out?

7 – 3 = 4

You have just subtracted 3 from 7 .

How many circles are there?

How many are crossed out?

How many are left, that aren't crossed out?

☐ – ☐ = ☐

I have just subtracted ☐ from ☐ .

How many diamonds are there?

How many are crossed out?

How many are left, that aren't crossed out?

[ ] − [ ] = [ ]

I have just subtracted [ ] from [ ] .

How many hearts are there?

How many are crossed out?

How many are left, that aren't crossed out?

[ ] − [ ] = [ ]

I have just subtracted [ ] from [ ] .

Practice subtracting.

Count out the objects in each group. Then cross 3 out. How many are left? Remember, don't count the ones you crossed out.

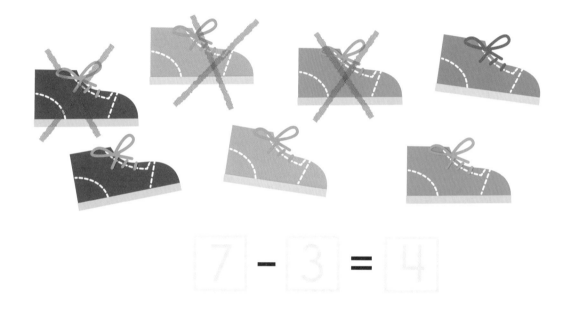

7 - 3 = 4

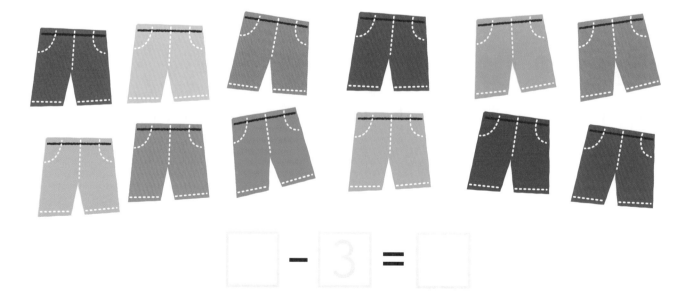

☐ - 3 = ☐

□ − 3 = □

□ − 3 = □

□ − 3 = □

The place of each digit in a number determines its value.

tens	ones
1	6

10 + 6 = 16

The 6 in 16 means 6 ones.

The 1 in 16 means 1 ten.

tens	ones
2	1

20 + 1 = 21

The 1 in 21 means 1 one.

The 2 in 21 means 2 tens.

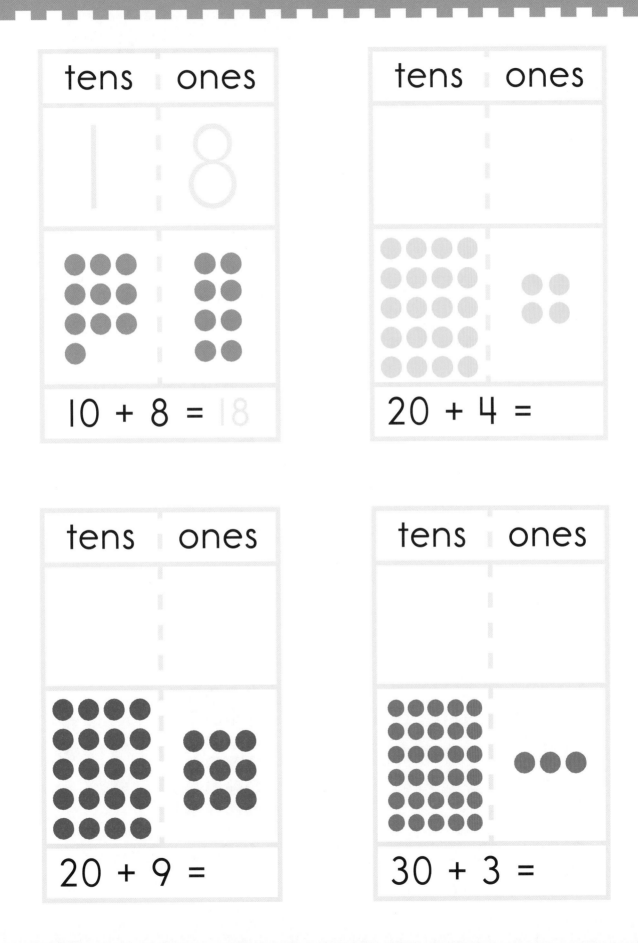

tens	ones
1	8

10 + 8 = 18

tens	ones

20 + 4 =

tens	ones

20 + 9 =

tens	ones

30 + 3 =

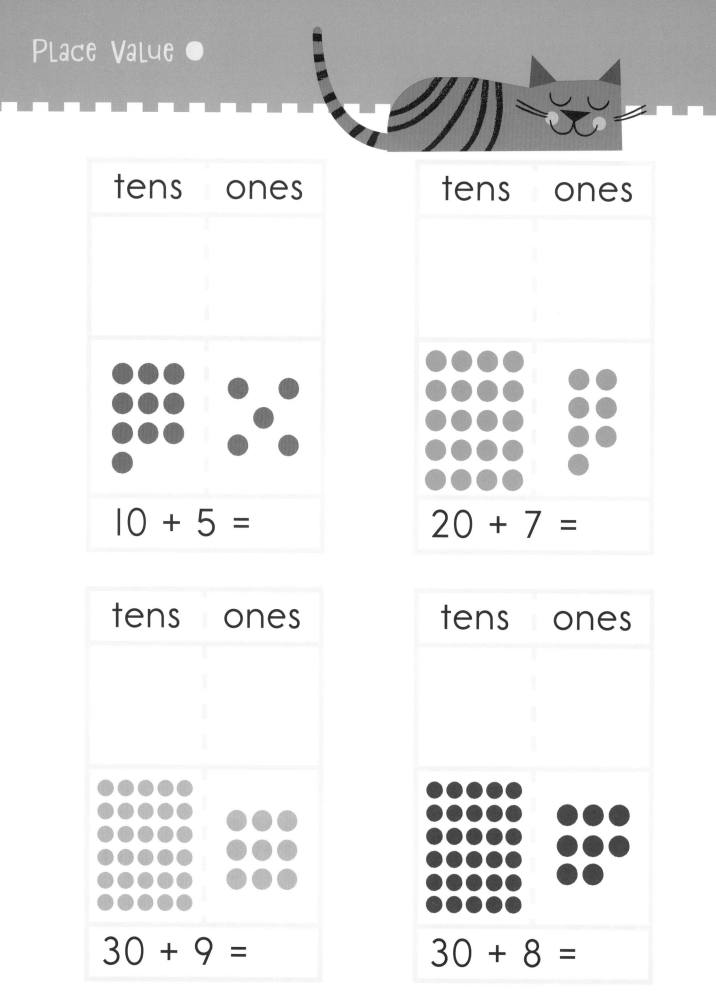

tens	ones

10 + 5 =

tens	ones

20 + 7 =

tens	ones

30 + 9 =

tens	ones

30 + 8 =

35

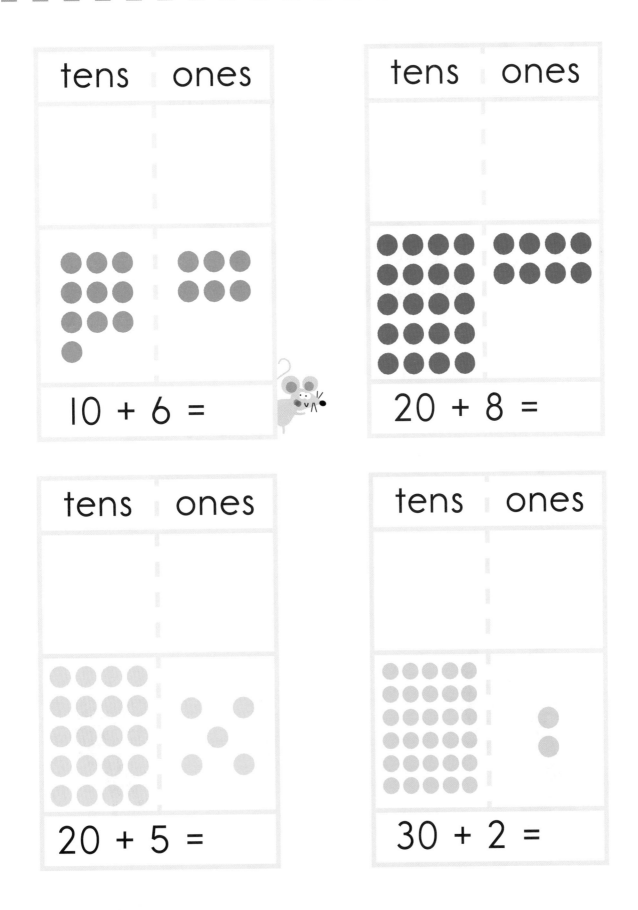

tens	ones

10 + 6 =

tens	ones

20 + 8 =

tens	ones

20 + 5 =

tens	ones

30 + 2 =

Which is bigger?
Circle the biggest object in each row.

Which is smaller?

Circle the smallest object in each row.

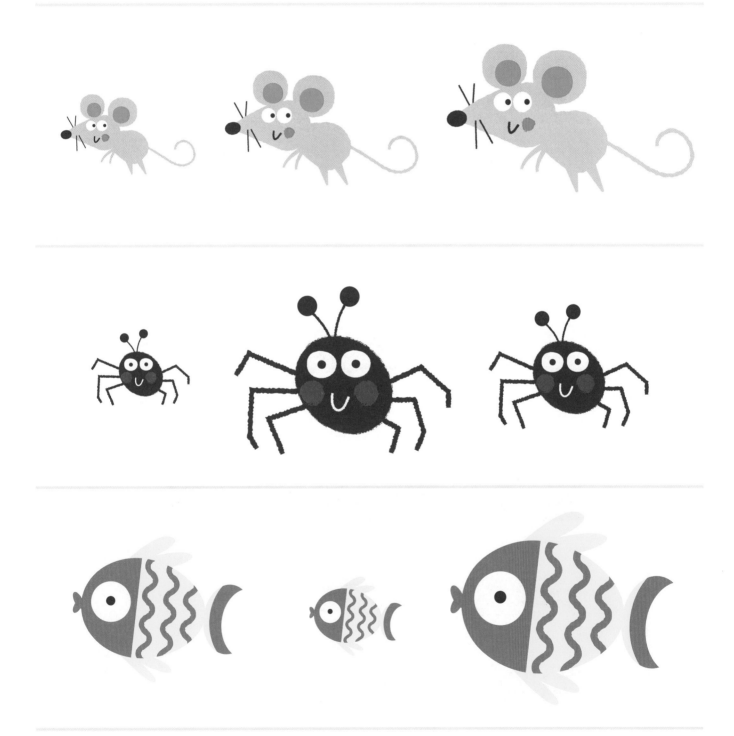

Which is longer?

Circle the longest one in each group.

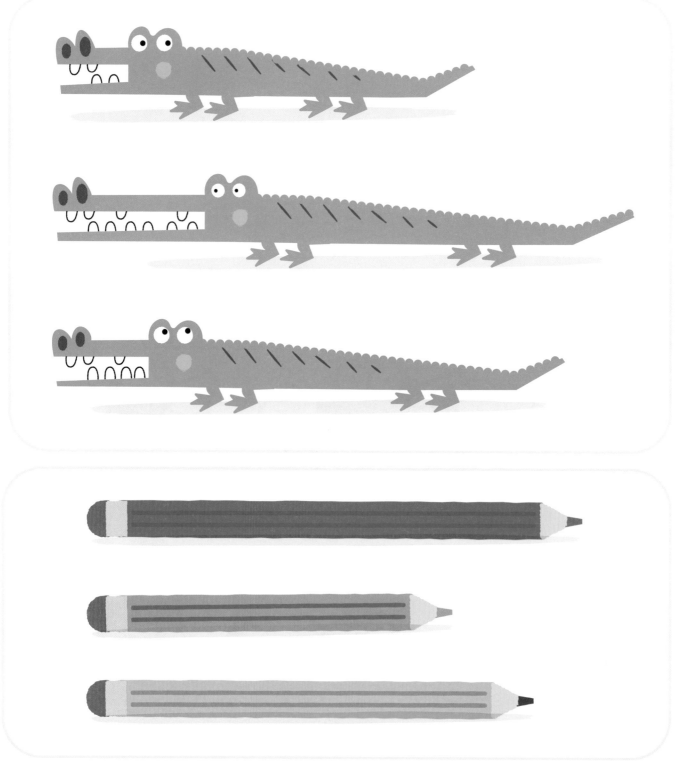

Which is shorter?

Circle the shortest one in each group.

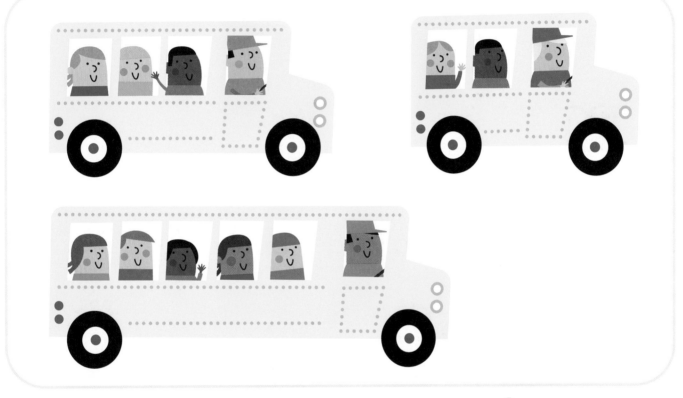

Draw a snake that is longer.

Draw a toucan with a longer beak.

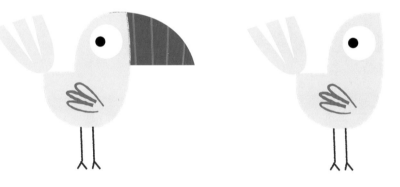

Draw a puppet with a longer nose.

Draw a caterpillar that is shorter.

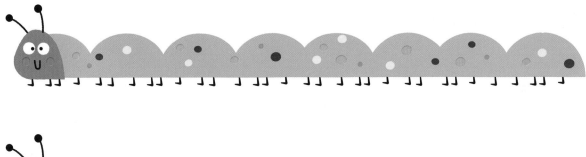

Draw a mouse with a shorter tail.

Draw a cat with shorter whiskers.

Which of these things are the same?
Circle the ones in each row that are the same.

Which of these things are different?
Circle the thing in each row that is different.

Learn the names of shapes.

Circle the correct shape in each row.

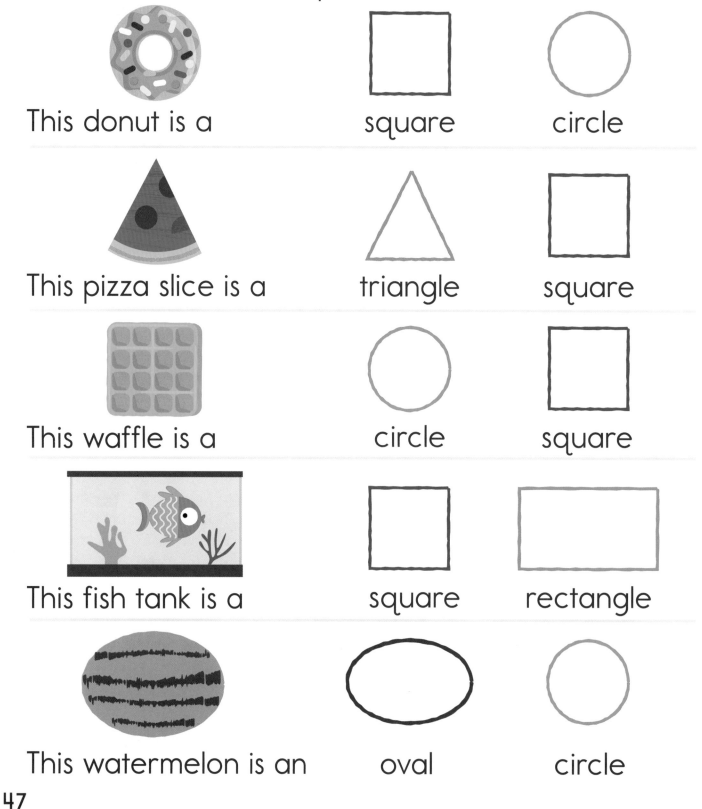

This donut is a   square   circle

This pizza slice is a   triangle   square

This waffle is a   circle   square

This fish tank is a   square   rectangle

This watermelon is an   oval   circle

Circle the shape that is different in each group.

Practice drawing shapes.

circle   Trace a circle.   Draw a circle.

triangle   Trace a triangle.   Draw a triangle.

square   Trace a square.   Draw a square.

rectangle Trace a rectangle. Draw a rectangle.

oval Trace an oval. Draw an oval.

Dog

The dog is **inside** the dog house.

The cat is **on** the chair.

The frog is **under** the cat.

The bird house is **above** the dog house.

Circle the correct answer for each sentence.

The alien is _____ the spaceship.

inside   **outside**

The alien is flying _____ the moon.

under   **over**

The astronaut is _____ the spaceship.

outside   **inside**

The astronaut is _____ the moon.

under   **over**

Describe where the objects are.

The mouse is behind the _____.   **square**   **triangle**

The frog is under the _____.   **circle**   **oval**

The mushroom is above the _____. **rectangle** **oval**

The spider is inside the _____.   **triangle**   **square**

55

Color the shapes.

circle	triangle	square	rectangle	oval
orange	blue	yellow	green	purple

Congratulations!

You know your numbers, you are learning to add and subtract and to recognize shapes, and you've learned about length and position words.

Good work!

Name

Date

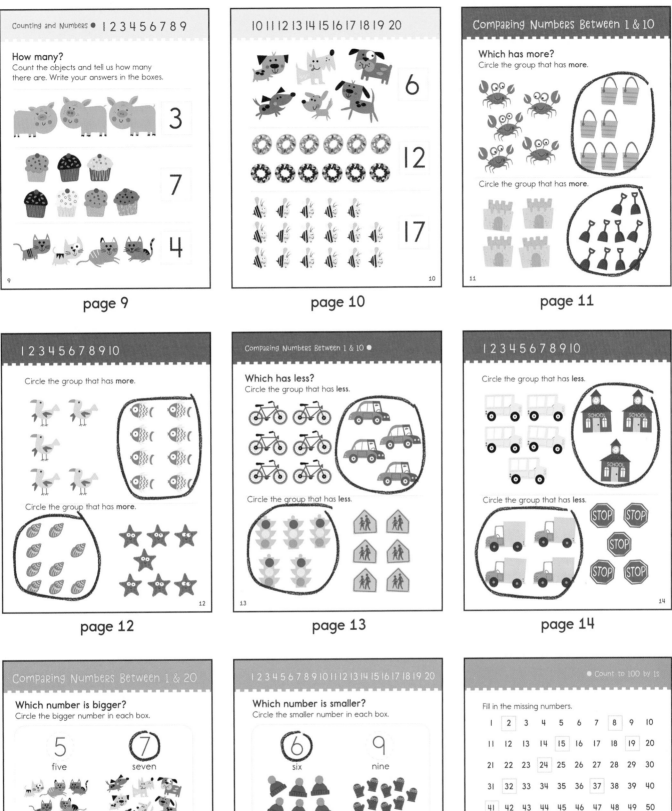

page 9

page 10

page 11

page 12

page 13

page 14

page 15

page 16

page 18

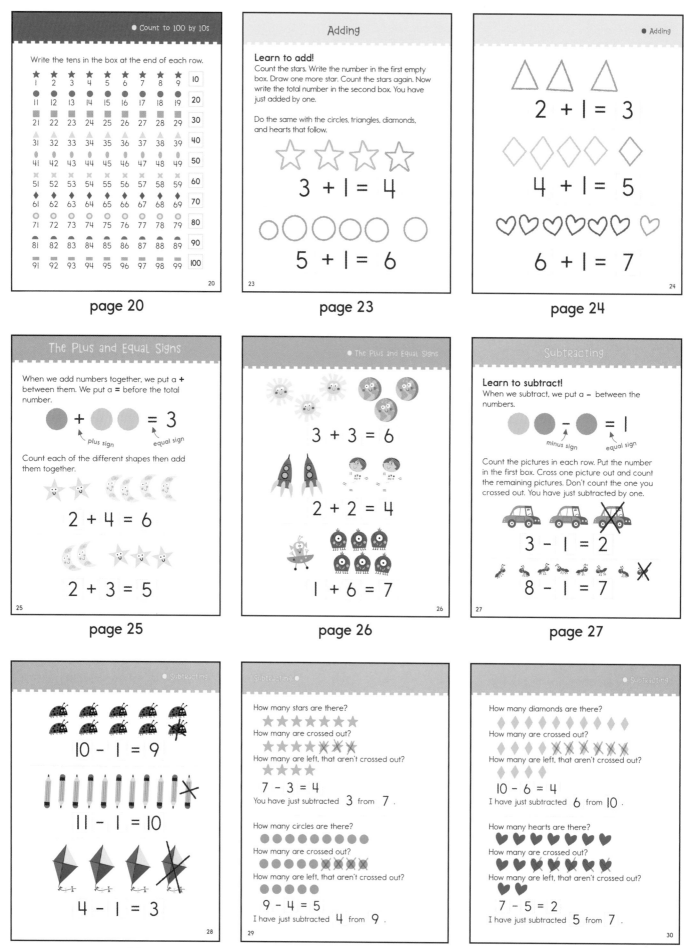

page 20

page 23

page 24

page 25

page 26

page 27

page 28

page 29

page 30

59

Practice subtracting.
Count out the objects in each group. Then cross 3 out. How many are left? Remember, don't count the ones you crossed out.

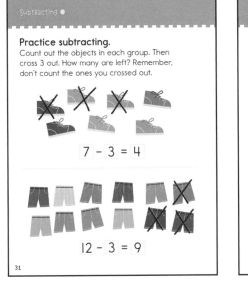

$7 - 3 = 4$

$12 - 3 = 9$

31

page 31

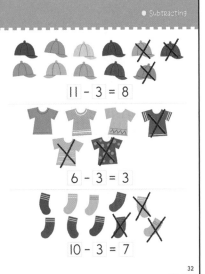

$11 - 3 = 8$

$6 - 3 = 3$

$10 - 3 = 7$

32

page 32

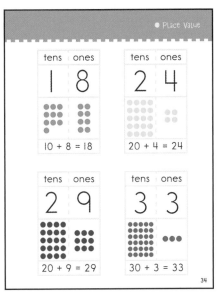

tens	ones
1	8

$10 + 8 = 18$

tens	ones
2	4

$20 + 4 = 24$

tens	ones
2	9

$20 + 9 = 29$

tens	ones
3	3

$30 + 3 = 33$

34

page 34

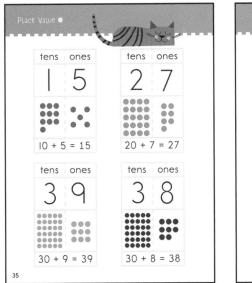

tens	ones
1	5

$10 + 5 = 15$

tens	ones
2	7

$20 + 7 = 27$

tens	ones
3	9

$30 + 9 = 39$

tens	ones
3	8

$30 + 8 = 38$

35

page 35

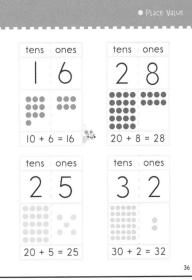

tens	ones
1	6

$10 + 6 = 16$

tens	ones
2	8

$20 + 8 = 28$

tens	ones
2	5

$20 + 5 = 25$

tens	ones
3	2

$30 + 2 = 32$

36

page 36

Comparing Size

Which is bigger?
Circle the biggest object in each row.

page 37

Which is smaller?
Circle the smallest object in each row.

38

page 38

Comparing Length

Which is longer?
Circle the longest one in each group.

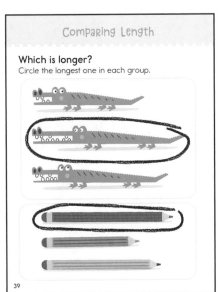

39

page 39

Which is shorter?
Circle the shortest one in each group.

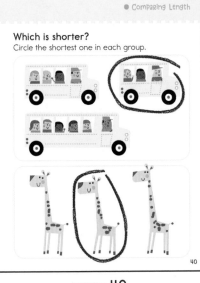

40

page 40

page 43

Classifying Objects

Which of these things are the same?
Circle the ones in each row that are the same.

43

---

page 44

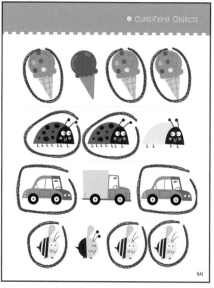

Classifying Objects

44

---

page 45

Classifying Objects

Which of these things are different?
Circle the thing in each row that is different.

45

---

page 46

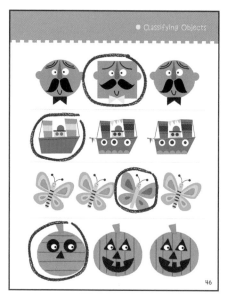

Classifying Objects

46

---

page 47

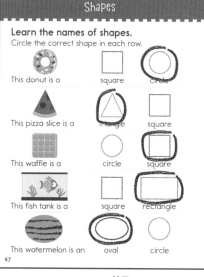

Shapes

Learn the names of shapes.
Circle the correct shape in each row.

This donut is a — square — circle

This pizza slice is a — triangle — square

This waffle is a — circle — square

This fish tank is a — square — rectangle

This watermelon is an — oval — circle

47

---

page 48

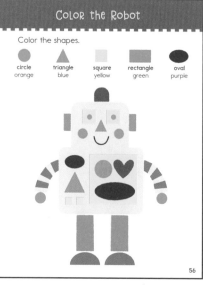

Shapes

Circle the shape that is different in each group.

48

---

page 54

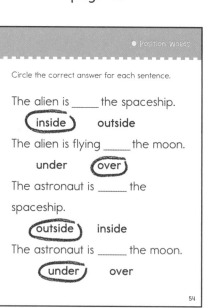

Position Words

Circle the correct answer for each sentence.

The alien is _____ the spaceship.
inside — outside

The alien is flying _____ the moon.
under — **over**

The astronaut is _____ the spaceship.
outside — inside

The astronaut is _____ the moon.
under — over

54

---

page 55

Position Words

Describe where the objects are.
The mouse is behind the _____. — square — **triangle**
The frog is under the _____. — circle — **oval**
The mushroom is above the _____. — **rectangle** — oval
The spider is inside the _____. — triangle — **square**

55

---

page 56

Color the Robot

Color the shapes.

circle — orange
triangle — blue
square — yellow
rectangle — green
oval — purple

56
